U.S. Department
of Transportation

**Federal Aviation
Administration**

# PRIVATE PILOT

## Practical Test Standards

### for

## AIRPLANE
### (MEL and MES)

## August 2002

**FLIGHT STANDARDS SERVICE
Washington, DC 20591**

# PRIVATE PILOT
# AIRPLANE

## Practical Test Standards

**2002**

**FLIGHT STANDARDS SERVICE**
Washington, DC 20591

# NOTE

Material in FAA-S-8081-14A will be effective August 1, 2002. All previous editions of the Private Pilot—Airplane Practical Test Standards will be obsolete as of this date.

# FOREWORD

The Private Pilot—Airplane Practical Test Standards (PTS) book has been published by the Federal Aviation Administration (FAA) to establish the standards for the private pilot certification practical tests for the airplane category, multiengine land and sea class. FAA inspectors and designated pilot examiners shall conduct practical tests in compliance with these standards. Flight instructors and applicants should find these standards helpful during training and when preparing for the practical test.

/s/ 4/23/2002

---

Joseph K. Tintera, Manager
Regulatory Support Division
Flight Standards Service

# CONTENTS

# INTRODUCTION

## General Information

The Flight Standards Service of the Federal Aviation Administration (FAA) has developed this practical test book as the standard that shall be used by FAA inspectors and designated pilot examiners when conducting private pilot—airplane practical tests. Flight instructors are expected to use this book when preparing applicants for practical tests. Applicants should be familiar with this book and refer to these standards during their training.

Information considered directive in nature is described in this practical test book in terms, such as "shall" and "must" indicating the actions are mandatory. Guidance information is described in terms, such as "should" and "may" indicating the actions are desirable or permissive, but not mandatory.

The FAA gratefully acknowledges the valuable assistance provided by many individuals and organizations throughout the aviation community who contributed their time and talent in assisting with the revision of these practical test standards.

This practical test standard may be downloaded from the Regulatory Support Division's, AFS-600, web site at http://afs600.faa.gov. Subsequent changes to this standard, in accordance with AC 60-27, Announcement of Availability: Changes to Practical Test Standards, will also be available on AFS-600's web site and then later incorporated into a printed revision.

This publication can be purchased from the Superintendent of Documents, U.S. Government Printing Office, Washington, DC 20402.

Comments regarding this publication should be sent to:

U.S. Department of Transportation
Federal Aviation Administration
Flight Standards Service
Airman Testing Standards Branch, AFS-630
P.O. Box 25082
Oklahoma City, OK 73125

*FAA-S-8081-14A*

## Practical Test Standards Concept

Title 14 of the Code of Federal Regulations (14 CFR) part 61 specifies the AREAS OF OPERATION in which knowledge and skill must be demonstrated by the applicant before the issuance of a private pilot certificate or rating. The CFRs provide the flexibility to permit the FAA to publish practical test standards containing the AREAS OF OPERATION and specific TASKs in which pilot competency shall be demonstrated. The FAA shall revise this book whenever it is determined that changes are needed in the interest of safety. *Adherence to the provisions of the regulations and the practical test standards is mandatory for the evaluation of private pilot applicants.*

## Practical Test Book Description

This test book contains the following Private Pilot—Airplane Practical Test Standards:

> Airplane—Multiengine Land and Sea

The Private Pilot—Airplane Practical Test Standards includes the AREAS OF OPERATION and TASKs for the issuance of an initial private pilot certificate and for the addition of category ratings and/or class ratings to that certificate.

## Practical Test Standards Description

AREAS OF OPERATION are phases of the practical test arranged in a logical sequence within each standard. They begin with Preflight Preparation and end with Postflight Procedures. The examiner, however, may conduct the practical test in any sequence that will result in a complete and efficient test; *however, the ground portion of the practical test shall be accomplished before the flight portion.*

TASKs are titles of knowledge areas, flight procedures, or maneuvers appropriate to an AREA OF OPERATION. The abbreviation(s) within parentheses immediately following a TASK refer to the category and/or class aircraft appropriate to that TASK. The meaning of each abbreviation is as follows.

| | |
|---|---|
| **AMEL** | Airplane—Multiengine Land |
| **AMES** | Airplane—Multiengine Sea |

**NOTE:** When administering a test based on this PTS, the TASKs appropriate to the class airplane (AMEL or AMES) used for the test shall be included in the plan of action. The absence of a class indicates the TASK is for all classes.

NOTE is used to emphasize special considerations required in the AREA OF OPERATION or TASK.

REFERENCE identifies the publication(s) that describe(s) the TASK. Descriptions of TASKs are not included in these standards because this information can be found in the current issue of the listed reference. Publications other than those listed may be used for references if their content conveys substantially the same meaning as the referenced publications.

These practical test standards are based on the following references.

| | |
|---|---|
| **14 CFR part 43** | Maintenance, Preventive Maintenance, Rebuilding, and Alteration |
| **14 CFR part 61** | Certification: Pilots, Flight Instructors, and Ground Instructors |
| **14 CFR part 91** | General Operating and Flight Rules |
| **AC 00-6** | Aviation Weather |
| **AC 00-45** | Aviation Weather Services |
| **AC 61-23/ FAA-H-8083-25** | Pilot's Handbook of Aeronautical Knowledge |
| **AC 61-65** | Certification: Pilots and Flight Instructors |
| **AC 61-67** | Stall and Spin Awareness Training. |
| **AC 61-84** | Role of Preflight Preparation |
| **AC 90-48** | Pilots' Role in Collision Avoidance |
| **AC 90-66** | Recommended Standard Traffic Patterns and Practices for Aeronautical Operations At Airports Without Operating Control Towers |
| **AC 91-69** | Seaplane Safety for FAR Part 91 Operations |
| **AC 120-51** | Crew Resource Management Training |
| **FAA-H-8083-1** | Aircraft Weight and Balance Handbook |
| **FAA-H-8083-3** | Airplane Flying Handbook |
| **FAA-H-8083-15** | Instrument Flying Handbook |
| **AIM** | Aeronautical Information Manual |
| **AFD** | Airport Facility Directory |
| **NOTAMs** | Notices to Airmen |
| **Other** | Pilot Operating Handbook |
| | FAA-Approved Flight Manual |
| | Navigation Charts |
| | Seaplane Supplement |

The Objective lists the elements that must be satisfactorily performed to demonstrate competency in a TASK. The Objective includes:

1.  specifically what the applicant should be able to do;
2.  conditions under which the TASK is to be performed; and
3.  acceptable performance standards.

## Use of the Practical Test Standards Book

The FAA requires that all private pilot practical tests be conducted in accordance with the appropriate private practical test standards and the policies set forth in the INTRODUCTION. Applicants shall be evaluated in **ALL** TASKS included in each AREA OF OPERATION of the appropriate practical test standard, unless otherwise noted.

An applicant, who holds at least a private pilot certificate seeking an additional airplane category rating and/or class rating at the private pilot level, shall be evaluated in the AREAS OF OPERATION and TASKS listed in the Additional Rating Task Table. At the discretion of the examiner, an evaluation of the applicant's competence in the remaining AREAS OF OPERATION and TASKs may be conducted.

If the applicant holds two or more category or class ratings at least at the private level, and the ratings table indicates differing required TASKS, the "least restrictive" entry applies. For example, if "ALL" and "NONE" are indicated for one AREA OF OPERATION, the "NONE" entry applies. If "B" and "B, C" are indicated, the "B" entry applies.

In preparation for each practical test, the examiner shall develop a written "plan of action." The "plan of action" shall include all TASKs in each AREA OF OPERATION, unless noted otherwise. If the elements in one TASK have already been evaluated in another TASK, they need not be repeated. For example, the "plan of action" need not include evaluating the applicant on complying with markings, signals, and clearances at the end of the flight, if that element was sufficiently observed at the beginning of the flight. *Any TASK selected for evaluation during a practical test shall be evaluated in its entirety.*

The examiner is not required to follow the precise order in which the AREAS OF OPERATION and TASKs appear in this book. The examiner may change the sequence or combine TASKs with similar Objectives to have an orderly and efficient flow of the practical test. For example, Radio Communications and ATC Light Signals may be combined with Traffic Patterns. The examiner's "plan of action" shall include the order and combination of TASKs to be demonstrated by the applicant in a manner that will result in an efficient and valid test.

The examiner is expected to use good judgment in the performance of simulated emergency procedures. The use of the safest means for simulation is expected. Consideration must be given to local conditions, both meteorological and topographical, at the time of the test, as well as the applicant's workload, and the condition of the aircraft used. If the procedure being evaluated would jeopardize safety, it is expected that the applicant will simulate that portion of the maneuver.

## Special Emphasis Areas

Examiners shall place special emphasis upon areas of aircraft operations considered critical to flight safety. Among these are:

1. positive aircraft control;
2. procedures for positive exchange of flight controls (who is flying the airplane);
3. stall/spin awareness;
4. collision avoidance;
5. wake turbulence avoidance;
6. Land and Hold Short Operations (LAHSO);
7. runway incursion avoidance;
8. controlled flight into terrain (CFIT);
9. aeronautical decision making (ADM);
10. checklist usage; and
11. other areas deemed appropriate to any phase of the practical test.

Although these areas may not be specifically addressed under each **TASK, they are essential to flight safety and will be evaluated during the** practical test. In all instances, the applicant's actions will relate to the complete situation.

## Removal of the "Airplane Multiengine VFR Only" Limitation

The removal of the "Airplane Multiengine VFR Only" limitation, at the private pilot certificate level, requires an applicant to satisfactorily perform the following AREAS OF OPERATION and TASKs from the private AMEL and AMES PTS in a multiengine airplane that has a manufacturer's published $V_{MC}$ speed.

AREA OF OPERATION XI: MULTIENGINE OPERATIONS

TASK C: ENGINE FAILURE DURING FLIGHT
(By Reference to Instruments)
TASK D: INSTRUMENT APPROACH—ONE ENGINE
INOPERATIVE (By Reference to Instruments)

## Removal of the "Limited to Center Thrust" Limitation

The removal of the "Limited to Center Thrust" limitation at the private pilot certificate level requires an applicant to satisfactorily perform the following AREAS OF OPERATION and TASKs from the private AMEL and AMES PTS in a multiengine airplane that has a manufacturer's published $V_{MC}$ speed.

AREA OF OPERATION I:  PREFLIGHT PREPARTATION

    TASK H:  PRINCIPLES OF FLIGHT-ENGINE INOPERATIVE

AREA OF OPERATION X: EMERGENCY OPERATIONS

    TASK B:  ENGINE FAILURE DURING TAKEOFF BEFORE Vmc (SIMULATED)
    TASK C:  ENGINE FAILURE AFTER LIFT-OFF (SIMULATED)
    TASK D:  APPROACH AND LANDING WITH AN INOPERATIVE ENGINE (SIMULATED)

AREA OF OPERATION XI: MULTIENGINE OPERATIONS

    TASK A:  MANEUVERING WITH ONE ENGINE INOPERATIVE
    TASK B:  $V_{MC}$ DEMONSTRATION)

## Private Pilot—Airplane Practical Test Prerequisites

An applicant for the Private Pilot—Airplane Practical Test is required by 14 CFR part 61 to:

1. be at least 17 years of age;
2. be able to read, speak, write, and understand the English language. If there is a doubt, use AC 60-28, English Language Skill Standards;
3. have passed the appropriate private pilot knowledge test since the beginning of the 24th month before the month in which he or she takes the practical test;
4. have satisfactorily accomplished the required training and obtained the aeronautical experience prescribed;
5. possess at least a current third class medical certificate;
6. have an endorsement from an authorized instructor certifying that the applicant has received and logged training time within 60 days preceding the date of application in preparation for the practical test, and is prepared for the practical test; and
7. also have an endorsement certifying that the applicant has demonstrated satisfactory knowledge of the subject areas in which the applicant was deficient on the airman knowledge test.

## Aircraft and Equipment Required for the Practical Test

The private pilot—airplane applicant is required by 14 CFR section 61.45, to provide an airworthy, certificated aircraft for use during the practical test. This section further requires that the aircraft must:

1. be of U.S., foreign or military registry of the same category, class, and type, if applicable, for the certificate and/or rating for which the applicant is applying;
2. have fully functioning dual controls, except as provided for in 14 CFR section 61.45(c) and (e); and
3. be capable of performing all AREAS OF OPERATION appropriate to the rating sought and have no operating limitations, which prohibit its use in any of the AREAS OF OPERATION, required for the practical test.

## Flight Instructor Responsibility

An appropriately rated flight instructor is responsible for training the private pilot applicant to acceptable standards in **all** subject matter areas, procedures, and maneuvers included in the TASKs within each AREA OF OPERATION in the appropriate private pilot practical test standard.

Because of the impact of their teaching activities in developing safe, proficient pilots, flight instructors should exhibit a high level of knowledge, skill, and the ability to impart that knowledge and skill to students.

Throughout the applicant's training, the flight instructor is responsible for emphasizing the performance of effective visual scanning and collision avoidance procedures.

## Examiner[1] Responsibility

The examiner conducting the practical test is responsible for determining that the applicant meets the acceptable standards of knowledge and skill of each TASK within the appropriate practical test standard. Since there is no formal division between the "oral" and "skill" portions of the practical test, this becomes an ongoing process throughout the test. Oral questioning, to determine the applicant's knowledge of TASKs and related safety factors, should be used judiciously at all times, especially during the flight portion of the practical test. Examiner's shall test to the greatest extent practicable

---

[1] The word "examiner" is used throughout the standards to denote either the FAA inspector or FAA designated pilot examiner who conducts an official practical test.

*FAA-S-8081-14A*

the applicant's correlative abilities rather than mere rote enumeration of facts throughout the practical test.

If the examiner determines that a TASK is incomplete, or the outcome uncertain, the examiner may require the applicant to repeat that TASK, or portions of that TASK. This provision has been made in the interest of fairness and does not mean that instruction, practice, or the repeating of an unsatisfactory task is permitted during the certification process. When practical, the remaining TASKs of the practical test phase should be completed before repeating the questionable TASK.

On multiengine practical tests where the failure of the most critical engine after lift off is required, the examiner must give consideration to local atmospheric conditions, terrain, and type of aircraft used. However the failure of an engine shall not be simulated until attaining at least $V_{SSE}/V_{YSE}$ and at an altitude not lower than 200 feet AGL.

During simulated engine failures on multiengine practical tests the examiner shall set zero thrust after the applicant has simulated feathering the propeller. The examiner shall require the applicant to demonstrate at least one landing with a simulated-feathered propeller with the engine set to zero thrust.

Throughout the flight portion of the practical test, the examiner shall evaluate the applicant's use of visual scanning and collision avoidance procedures.

**Satisfactory Performance**

Satisfactory performance to meet the requirements for certification is based on the applicant's ability to safely:

1. perform the TASKs specified in the AREAS OF OPERATION for the certificate or rating sought within the approved standards;
2. demonstrate mastery of the aircraft with the successful outcome of each TASK performed never seriously in doubt;
3. demonstrate satisfactory proficiency and competency within the approved standards;
4. demonstrate sound judgment; and
5. demonstrate single-pilot competence if the aircraft is type certificated for single-pilot operations.

## Unsatisfactory Performance

The tolerances represent the performance expected in good flying conditions. If, in the judgment of the examiner, the applicant does not meet the standards of performance of any TASK performed, the associated AREA OF OPERATION is failed and therefore, the practical test is failed.

The examiner or applicant may discontinue the test at any time when the failure of an AREA OF OPERATION makes the applicant ineligible for the certificate or rating sought. *The test may be continued ONLY with the consent of the applicant.* If the test is discontinued, the applicant is entitled credit for only those AREAS OF OPERATION and their associated TASKs satisfactorily performed. However, during the retest, and at the discretion of the examiner, any TASK may be re-evaluated, including those previously passed.

Typical areas of unsatisfactory performance and grounds for disqualification are:

1. Any action or lack of action by the applicant that requires corrective intervention by the examiner to maintain safe flight.
2. Failure to use proper and effective visual scanning techniques to clear the area before and while performing maneuvers.
3. Consistently exceeding tolerances stated in the Objectives.
4. Failure to take prompt corrective action when tolerances are exceeded.

When a notice of disapproval is issued, the examiner shall record the applicant's unsatisfactory performance in terms of the AREA OF OPERATION and specific TASK(s) not meeting the standard appropriate to the practical test conducted. The AREA(s) OF OPERATION/TASK(s) not tested and the number of practical test failures shall also be recorded. If the applicant fails the practical test because of a special emphasis area, the Notice of Disapproval shall indicate the associated TASK. i. e.: AREA OF OPERATION VIII, Maneuvering During Slow Flight, failure to use proper collision avoidance procedures.

## Crew Resource Management (CRM)

CRM refers to the effective use of all available resources: human resources, hardware, and information. Human resources include all groups routinely working with the cockpit crew or pilot who are involved with decisions that are required to operate a flight safely. These groups include, but are not limited to dispatchers, cabin crewmembers, maintenance personnel, air traffic controllers, and weather services. CRM is not a single TASK, but a set of competencies that must be evident in all TASKs in this practical test standard as applied to either single pilot operations or crew.

## Applicant's Use of Checklists

Throughout the practical test, the applicant is evaluated on the use of an appropriate checklist. Proper use is dependent on the specific TASK being evaluated. The situation may be such that the use of the checklist, while accomplishing elements of an Objective, would be either unsafe or impractical, especially in a single-pilot operation. In this case, a review of the checklist after the elements have been accomplished, would be appropriate. Division of attention and proper visual scanning should be considered when using a checklist.

## Use of Distractions During Practical Tests

Numerous studies indicate that many accidents have occurred when the pilot has been distracted during critical phases of flight. To evaluate the applicant's ability to utilize proper control technique while dividing attention both inside and/or outside the cockpit, the examiner shall cause realistic distractions during the flight portion of the practical test to evaluate the applicant's ability to divide attention while maintaining safe flight.

## Positive Exchange of Flight Controls

During flight training, there must always be a clear understanding between students and flight instructors of who has control of the aircraft. Prior to flight, a briefing should be conducted that includes the procedure for the exchange of flight controls. A positive three-step process in the exchange of flight controls between pilots is a proven procedure and one that is strongly recommended.

When the instructor wishes the student to take control of the aircraft, he or she will say, "You have the flight controls." The student acknowledges immediately by saying, "I have the flight controls." The flight instructor again says, "You have the flight controls." When control is returned to the instructor, follow the same procedure. A visual check is recommended to verify that the exchange has occurred. There should never by any doubt as to who is flying the aircraft.

## Metric Conversion Initiative

To assist pilots in understanding and using the metric measurement system, the practical test standards refer to the metric equivalent of various altitudes throughout. The inclusion of meters is intended to familiarize pilots with its use. The metric altimeter is arranged in 10 meter increments; therefore, when converting from feet to meters, the exact conversion, being too exact for practical purposes, is rounded to the nearest 10 meter increment or even altitude as necessary.

# PRIVATE PILOT—AIRPLANE

## Multiengine Land

### and

## Multiengine Sea

# CONTENTS

## Airplane Multiengine Land
## and
## Airplane Multiengine Sea

# ADDITIONAL RATING TASK TABLE

## Airplane Multiengine Land

<table>
<tr><td colspan="9">Addition of an Airplane Multiengine Land Rating<br>to an existing Private Pilot Certificate</td></tr>
<tr><td colspan="9">Required TASKs are indicated by either the TASK letter(s) that apply(s)<br>or an indication that all or none of the TASKs must be tested based on<br>the notes in each AREA OF OPERATION.</td></tr>
<tr><td colspan="9">PRIVATE PILOT RATING(S) HELD</td></tr>
<tr><td>AREAS OF OPER-ATION</td><td>ASEL</td><td>ASES</td><td>AMES</td><td>RH</td><td>RG</td><td>Glider</td><td>Balloon</td><td>Airship</td></tr>
<tr><td>I</td><td>F,G,H</td><td>F,G,H</td><td>F,G</td><td>F,G,H</td><td>F,G,H</td><td>F,G,H</td><td>F,G,H</td><td>F,G,H</td></tr>
<tr><td>II</td><td>ALL</td><td>ALL</td><td>D</td><td>ALL</td><td>ALL</td><td>ALL</td><td>ALL</td><td>ALL</td></tr>
<tr><td>III</td><td>NONE</td><td>C</td><td>C</td><td>B,C</td><td>NONE</td><td>B,C</td><td>B,C</td><td>B,C</td></tr>
<tr><td>IV</td><td>A,B,C,D</td><td>A,B,C,D</td><td>A,B,C,D</td><td>A,B,C,D,K</td><td>A,B,C,D,K</td><td>A,B,C,D,K</td><td>A,B,C,D,K</td><td>A,B,C,D,K</td></tr>
<tr><td>V</td><td>ALL</td><td>ALL</td><td>NONE</td><td>ALL</td><td>ALL</td><td>ALL</td><td>ALL</td><td>ALL</td></tr>
<tr><td>VI</td><td>NONE</td><td>NONE</td><td>NONE</td><td>ALL</td><td>NONE</td><td>ALL</td><td>ALL</td><td>ALL</td></tr>
<tr><td>VII</td><td>NONE</td><td>NONE</td><td>NONE</td><td>NONE</td><td>NONE</td><td>ALL</td><td>ALL</td><td>NONE</td></tr>
<tr><td>VIII</td><td>ALL</td><td>ALL</td><td>NONE</td><td>ALL</td><td>ALL</td><td>ALL</td><td>ALL</td><td>ALL</td></tr>
<tr><td>IX</td><td>NONE</td><td>NONE</td><td>NONE</td><td>ALL</td><td>ALL</td><td>ALL</td><td>ALL</td><td>ALL</td></tr>
<tr><td>X</td><td>ALL</td><td>ALL</td><td>B,D,E</td><td>ALL</td><td>ALL</td><td>ALL</td><td>ALL</td><td>ALL</td></tr>
<tr><td>XI</td><td>ALL</td><td>ALL</td><td>NONE</td><td>ALL</td><td>ALL</td><td>ALL</td><td>ALL</td><td>ALL</td></tr>
<tr><td>XII</td><td>NONE</td><td>NONE</td><td>NONE</td><td>NONE</td><td>NONE</td><td>ALL</td><td>ALL</td><td>ALL</td></tr>
<tr><td>XIII</td><td>NONE</td><td>A</td><td>A</td><td>A</td><td>A</td><td>A</td><td>A</td><td>A</td></tr>
</table>

FAA-S-8081-14A

# ADDITIONAL RATING TASK TABLE

## Airplane Multiengine Sea

| Addition of an Airplane Multiengine Sea Rating to an existing Private Pilot Certificate | | | | | | | | |
|---|---|---|---|---|---|---|---|---|
| Required TASKs are indicated by either the TASK letter(s) that apply(s) or an indication that all or none of the TASKs must be tested based on the notes in each AREA OF OPERATION. | | | | | | | | |
| **PRIVATE PILOT RATING(S) HELD** | | | | | | | | |
| AREAS OF OPER- ATION | **AMEL** | **ASEL** | **ASES** | **RH** | **RG** | **Glider** | **Balloon** | **Airship** |
| I | F,G,I,J | F,G,H, I,J | F,G,H | F,G,H, I,J | F,G,H, I,J | F,G,H, I,J | F,G,H, I,J | F,G,H, I,J |
| II | E | ALL | ALL | ALL | ALL | ALL | ALL | ALL |
| III | C | C | NONE | B,C | C | B,C | B,C | B,C |
| IV | A,B,C, D,E,F, G,H | A,B,C, D,E,F, G,H | A,B,C, D,E,F, G,H | ALL | ALL | ALL | ALL | ALL |
| V | NONE | ALL | ALL | ALL | ALL | ALL | ALL | ALL |
| VI | NONE | NONE | NONE | ALL | NONE | ALL | ALL | ALL |
| VII | NONE | NONE | NONE | NONE | NONE | ALL | ALL | NONE |
| VIII | NONE | ALL | ALL | ALL | ALL | ALL | ALL | ALL |
| IX | NONE | NONE | NONE | ALL | ALL | ALL | ALL | ALL |
| X | ALL | ALL | ALL | ALL | ALL | ALL | ALL | ALL |
| XI | NONE | ALL | ALL | ALL | ALL | ALL | ALL | ALL |
| XII | NONE | NONE | NONE | NONE | NONE | ALL | ALL | ALL |
| XIII | B,C,D | B,C,D | NONE | ALL | B,C,D | ALL | ALL | ALL |

FAA-S-8081-14A

# APPLICANT'S PRACTICAL TEST CHECKLIST

## APPOINTMENT WITH EXAMINER:

**EXAMINER'S NAME**_____

**LOCATION** _____

**DATE/TIME** _____

### ACCEPTABLE AIRCRAFT

Aircraft Documents:
Airworthiness Certificate
Registration Certificate
Operating Limitations
Aircraft Maintenance Records:
Logbook Record of Airworthiness Inspections
and AD Compliance
Pilot's Operating Handbook, FAA-Approved
Airplane Flight Manual

### PERSONAL EQUIPMENT

- ☐ View-Limiting Device
- ☐ Current Aeronautical Charts
- ☐ Computer and Plotter
- ☐ Flight Plan Form
- ☐ Flight Logs
- ☐ Current AIM, Airport Facility Directory, and Appropriate
Publications

### PERSONAL RECORDS

- ☐ Identification - Photo/Signature ID
- ☐ Pilot Certificate
- ☐ Current Medical Certificate
- ☐ Completed FAA Form 8710-1, Airman Certificate and/or
Rating Application with Instructor's Signature (if
applicable)
- ☐ Computer Test Report
- ☐ Pilot Logbook with appropriate Instructor Endorsements
- ☐ FAA Form 8060-5, Notice of Disapproval (if applicable)
- ☐ Approved School Graduation Certificate (if applicable)
- ☐ Examiner's Fee (if applicable)

*FAA-S-8081-14A*

# EXAMINER'S PRACTICAL TEST CHECKLIST

## Airplane Multiengine Land
## and
## Airplane Multiengine Sea

**APPLICANT'S NAME**_____

**LOCATION**_____

**DATE/TIME**_____

## I. PREFLIGHT PREPARATION

- ☐ **A.** Certificates and Documents (AMEL and AMES)
- ☐ **B.** Airworthiness Requirements (AMEL and AMES)
- ☐ **C.** Weather Information (AMEL and AMES)
- ☐ **D.** Cross-Country Flight Planning (AMEL and AMES)
- ☐ **E.** National Airspace System (AMEL and AMES)
- ☐ **F.** Performance and Limitations (AMEL and AMES)
- ☐ **G.** Operation of Systems (AMEL and AMES)
- ☐ **H.** Principles of Flight—Engine Inoperative (AMEL and AMES)
- ☐ **I.** Water and Seaplane Characteristics (AMES)
- ☐ **J.** Seaplane Bases, Maritime Rules, and Aids to Marine Navigation (AMES)
- ☐ **K.** Aeromedical Factors (AMEL and AMES)

## II. PREFLIGHT PROCEDURES

- ☐ **A.** Preflight Inspection (AMEL and AMES)
- ☐ **B.** Cockpit Management (AMEL and AMES)
- ☐ **C.** Engine Starting (AMEL and AMES)
- ☐ **D.** Taxiing (AMEL)
- ☐ **E.** Taxiing and Sailing (AMES)
- ☐ **F.** Before Takeoff Check (AMEL and AMES)

## III. AIRPORT AND SEAPLANE BASE OPERATIONS

- ☐ **A.** Radio Communications and ATC Light Signals (AMEL and AMES)
- ☐ **B.** Traffic Patterns (AMEL and AMES)
- ☐ **C.** Airport/Seaplane Base, Runway, and Taxiway Signs, Markings, and Lighting (AMEL and AMES)

## IV. TAKEOFFS, LANDINGS, AND GO-AROUNDS

☐ **A.** Normal and Crosswind Takeoff and Climb
(AMEL and AMES)
☐ **B.** Normal and Crosswind Approach and Landing
(AMEL and AMES)
☐ **C.** Short-Field Takeoff (Confined Area—AMEL) and
Maximum Performance Climb (AMEL and AMES)
☐ **D.** Short-Field (Confined Area—AMES) Approach
and Landing (AMEL and AMES)
☐ **E.** Glassy Water Takeoff and Climb (AMES)
☐ **F.** Glassy Water Approach and Landing (AMES)
☐ **G.** Rough Water Takeoff and Climb (AMES)
☐ **H.** Rough Water Approach and Landing (AMES)
☐ **I.** Go-Around/Rejected Landing (AMEL and AMES)

## V. PERFORMANCE MANEUVER

☐ Steep Turns (AMEL and AMES)

## VI. GROUND REFERENCE MANEUVERS

☐ **A.** Rectangular Course (AMEL and AMES)
☐ **B.** S-Turns (AMEL and AMES)
☐ **C.** Turns Around a Point (AMEL and AMES)

## VII. NAVIGATION

☐ **A.** Pilotage and Dead Reckoning (AMEL and AMES)
☐ **B.** Navigation Systems and Radar Services (AMEL and AMES)
☐ **C.** Diversion (AMEL and AMES)
☐ **D.** Lost Procedures (AMEL and AMES)

## VIII. SLOW FLIGHT AND STALLS

☐ **A.** Maneuvering During Slow Flight (AMEL and AMES)
☐ **B.** Power-Off Stalls (AMEL and AMES)
☐ **C.** Power-On Stalls (AMEL and AMES)
☐ **D.** Spin Awareness (AMEL and AMES)

## IX. BASIC INSTRUMENT MANEUVERS

☐ **A.** Straight-and-Level Flight (AMEL and AMES)
☐ **B.** Constant Airspeed Climbs (AMEL and AMES)
☐ **C.** Constant Speed Descents (AMEL and AMES)

☐ **D.** Turns to Headings (AMEL and AMES)
☐ **E.** Recovery from Unusual Flight Attitudes
☐ **F.** Radio Communications, Navigation System/Facilities, and
   Radar Services (AMEL and AMES)

## X. EMERGENCY OPERATIONS

☐ **A.** Emergency Descent (AMEL and AMES)
☐ **B.** Engine Failure During Takeoff Before $V_{MC}$ (Simulated)
   (AMEL and AMES)
☐ **C.** Engine Failure After Lift-Off (Simulated) (AMEL and AMES)
☐ **D.** Approach and Landing with an Inoperative Engine
   (Simulated) (AMEL and AMES)
☐ **E.** Systems and Equipment Malfunctions
   (AMEL and AMES)
☐ **F.** Emergency Equipment and Survival Gear (AMEL and AMES)

## XI. MULTIENGINE OPERATIONS

☐ **A.** Maneuvering with One Engine Inoperative
   (AMEL and AMES)
☐ **B.** $V_{MC}$ Demonstration (AMEL and AMES)
☐ **C.** Engine Failure During Flight (by Reference to
   Instruments) (AMEL and AMES)
☐ **D.** Instrument Approach—One Engine Inoperative
   (by Reference to Instruments) (AMEL and AMES)

## XII. NIGHT OPERATION

☐ Night Preparation (AMEL and AMES)

## XIII. POSTFLIGHT PROCEDURES

☐ **A.** After Landing, Parking, and Securing (AMEL and AMES)
☐ **B.** Anchoring (AMES)
☐ **C.** Docking and Mooring (AMES)
☐ **D.** Ramping/Beaching (AMES)

# I. AREA OF OPERATION: PREFLIGHT PREPARATION

## A. TASK: CERTIFICATES AND DOCUMENTS (AMEL and AMES)

**NOTE**: The examiner shall develop a scenario based on real time weather to evaluate TASKs C and D.

REFERENCES: 14 CFR parts 43, 61, 91; FAA-H-8083-3, AC 61-23/FAA-H-8083-25; POH/AFM.

**Objective.** To determine that the applicant exhibits knowledge of the elements related to certificates and documents by:

1. Explaining—

   a. private pilot certificate privileges, limitations and recent flight experience requirements.
   b. medical certificate, class and duration.
   c. pilot logbook or flight records.

2. Locating and explaining—

   a. airworthiness and registration certificates.
   b. operating limitations, placards, instrument markings, and POH/AFM.
   c. weight and balance data and equipment list.

## B. TASK: AIRWORTHINESS REQUIREMENTS (AMEL and AMES)

REFERENCES: 14 CFR part 91; AC 61-23/FAA-H-8083-25.

**Objective.** To determine that the applicant exhibits knowledge of the elements related to airworthiness requirements by:

1. Explaining—

   a. required instruments and equipment for day/night VFR.
   b. procedures and limitations for determining airworthiness of the airplane with inoperative instruments and equipment with and without an MEL.
   c. requirements and procedures for obtaining a special flight permit.

2. Locating and explaining—

   a. airworthiness directives.
   b. compliance records.
   c. maintenance/inspection requirements.
   d. appropriate record keeping.

## C. TASK: WEATHER INFORMATION (AMEL and AMES)

REFERENCES: 14 CFR part 91; AC 00-6, AC 00-45, AC 61-23/FAA-H-8083-25, AC 61-84; AIM.

**Objective.** To determine that the applicant:

1. Exhibits knowledge of the elements related to weather information by analyzing weather reports, charts, and forecasts from various sources with emphasis on—

   a. METAR, TAF, and FA.
   b. surface analysis chart.
   c. radar summary chart.
   d. winds and temperature aloft chart.
   e. significant weather prognostic charts.
   f. convective outlook chart.
   g. AWOS, ASOS, and ATIS reports.

2. Makes a competent "go/no-go" decision based on available weather information.

## D. TASK: CROSS-COUNTRY FLIGHT PLANNING (AMEL and AMES)

REFERENCES: 14 CFR part 91; AC 61-23/FAA-H-8083-25, AC 61-84; Navigation Charts; A/FD; AIM.

**Objective.** To determine that the applicant:

1. Exhibits knowledge of the elements related to cross-country flight planning by presenting and explaining a pre-planned VFR cross-country flight, as previously assigned by the examiner. On the day of the practical test, the final flight plan shall be to the first fuel stop, based on maximum allowable passengers, baggage and/or cargo loads using real-time weather.
2. Uses appropriate and current aeronautical charts.
3. Properly identifies airspace, obstructions, and terrain features.
4. Selects easily identifiable en route checkpoints.
5. Selects most favorable altitudes considering weather conditions and equipment capabilities.
6. Computes headings, flight time, and fuel requirements.
7. Selects appropriate navigation system/facilities and communication frequencies.
8. Applies pertinent information from NOTAMs, AF/D, and other flight publications.
9. Completes a navigation log and simulates filing a VFR flight plan.

**E. TASK: NATIONAL AIRSPACE SYSTEM** (AMEL and AMES)

REFERENCES: 14 CFR parts 71, 91; Navigation Charts; AIM.

**Objective.** To determine that the applicant exhibits knowledge of the elements related to the National Airspace System by explaining:

1. Basic VFR weather minimums—for all classes of airspace.
2. Airspace classes—their operating rules, pilot certification, and airplane equipment requirements for the following—

    a. Class A.
    b. Class B.
    c. Class C.
    d. Class D.
    e. Class E.
    f. Class G.

3. Special use and other airspace areas.

**F. TASK: PERFORMANCE AND LIMITATIONS** (AMEL and AMES)

REFERENCES: FAA-H-8083-1, AC 61-23/FAA-H-8083-25, AC 61-84; POH/AFM.

**Objective.** To determine that the applicant:

1. Exhibits knowledge of the elements related to performance and limitations by explaining the use of charts, tables, and data to determine performance and the adverse effects of exceeding limitations.
2. Computes weight and balance. Determines the computed weight and center of gravity is within the airplane's operating limitations and if the weight and center of gravity will remain within limits during all phases of flight.
3. Demonstrates use of the appropriate performance charts, tables, and data.
4. Describes the effects of atmospheric conditions on the airplane's performance.

## G. TASK: OPERATION OF SYSTEMS (AMEL and AMES)

REFERENCES: AC 61-23/FAA-H-8083-25; POH/AFM.

**Objective.** To determine that the applicant exhibits knowledge of the elements related to the operation of systems on the airplane provided for the flight test by explaining at least three (3) of the following systems:

1. Primary flight controls and trim.
2. Flaps, leading edge devices, and spoilers.
3. Water rudders (AMES).
4. Powerplant and propeller.
5. Landing gear.
6. Fuel, oil, and hydraulic.
7. Electrical.
8. Avionics.
9. Pitot-static vacuum/pressure, and associated flight instruments.
10. Environmental.
11. Deicing and anti-icing.

## H. TASK: PRINCIPLES OF FLIGHT—ENGINE INOPERATIVE
(AMEL and AMES)

REFERENCES: FAA-H-8083-3, AC 61-23/FAA-H-8083-25; POH/AFM.

**Objective.** To determine that the applicant exhibits knowledge of the elements related to engine inoperative principles of flight by explaining the:

1. meaning of the term "critical engine."
2. effects of density altitude on the $V_{MC}$ demonstration.
3. effects of airplane weight and center of gravity on control.
4. effects of angle of bank on $V_{MC}$.
5. relationship of $V_{MC}$ to stall speed.
6. reasons for loss of directional control.
7. indications of loss of directional control.
8. importance of maintaining the proper pitch and bank attitude, and the proper coordination of controls.
9. loss of directional control recovery procedure.
10. engine failure during takeoff including planning, decisions, and single-engine operations.

# I. TASK: WATER AND SEAPLANE CHARACTERISTICS (AMES)

REFERENCE: FAA-H-8083-3.

**Objective.** To determine that the applicant exhibits knowledge of the elements related to water and seaplane characteristics by explaining:

1. The characteristics of a water surface as affected by features, such as—

   a. size and location.
   b. protected and unprotected areas.
   c. surface wind.
   d. direction and strength of water current.
   e. floating and partially submerged debris.
   f. sandbars, islands, and shoals.
   g. vessel traffic and wakes.
   h. other features peculiar to the area.

2. Float and hull construction, and their effect on seaplane performance.
3. Causes of porpoising and skipping, and the pilot action required to prevent or correct these occurrences.

# J. TASK: SEAPLANE BASES, MARITIME RULES, AND AIDS TO MARINE NAVIGATION (AMES)

REFERENCES: FAA-H-8083-3; AIM.

**Objective.** To determine that the applicant exhibits knowledge of the elements related to seaplane bases, maritime rules, and aids to marine navigation by explaining:

1. How to locate and identify seaplane bases on charts or in directories.
2. Operating restrictions at various bases.
3. Right-of-way, steering, and sailing rules pertinent to seaplane operation.
4. Marine navigation aids such as buoys, beacons, lights, and sound signals.

**K. TASK: AEROMEDICAL FACTORS** (AMEL and AMES)

REFERENCES: AC 61-23/FAA-H-8083-25; AIM.

**Objective.** To determine that the applicant exhibits knowledge of the elements related to aeromedical factors by explaining:

1. The symptoms, causes, effects, and corrective actions of at least three (3) of the following—

   a. hypoxia.
   b. hyperventilation.
   c. middle ear and sinus problems.
   d. spatial disorientation.
   e. motion sickness.
   f. carbon monoxide poisoning.
   g. stress and fatigue.
   h. dehydration.

2. The effects of alcohol, drugs, and over-the-counter medications.
3. The effects of excess nitrogen during scuba dives upon a pilot or passenger in flight.

# II. AREA OF OPERATION: PREFLIGHT PROCEDURES

## A. TASK: PREFLIGHT INSPECTION (AMEL and AMES)

REFERENCES: FAA-H-8083-3; POH/AFM.

**Objective.** To determine that the applicant:

1. Exhibits knowledge of the elements related to preflight inspection. This shall include which items must be inspected, the reasons for checking each item, and how to detect possible defects.
2. Inspects the airplane with reference to an appropriate checklist.
3. Verifies the airplane is in condition for safe flight.

## B. TASK: COCKPIT MANAGEMENT (AMEL and AMES)

REFERENCES: FAA-H-8083-3; POH/AFM.

**Objective.** To determine that the applicant:

1. Exhibits knowledge of the elements related to cockpit management procedures.
2. Ensures all loose items in the cockpit and cabin are secured.
3. Organizes material and equipment in an efficient manner so they are readily available.
4. Briefs occupants on the use of safety belts, shoulder harnesses, doors, and emergency procedures.

## C. TASK: ENGINE STARTING (AMEL and AMES)

REFERENCES: FAA-H-8083-3, AC 61-23/FAA-H-8083-25, AC 91-13, AC 91-55; POH/AFM.

**Objective.** To determine that the applicant:

1. Exhibits knowledge of the elements related to recommended engine starting procedures. This shall include the use of an external power source, and starting under various atmospheric conditions.
2. Positions the airplane properly considering structures, surface conditions, other aircraft, and the safety of nearby persons and property.
3. Utilizes the appropriate checklist for starting procedure.

## D. TASK: TAXIING (AMEL)

REFERENCES: FAA-H-8083-3; POH/AFM.

**Objective.** To determine that the applicant:

1. Exhibits knowledge of the elements related to safe taxi procedures.
2. Performs a brake check immediately after the airplane begins moving.
3. Positions the flight controls properly for the existing wind conditions.
4. Controls direction and speed without excessive use of brakes.
5. Complies with airport/taxiway markings, signals, ATC clearances, and instructions.
6. Taxies so as to avoid other aircraft and hazards.

## E. TASK: TAXIING AND SAILING (AMES)

REFERENCES: FAA-H-8083-3; UCSG NAVIGATION RULES, INTERNATIONAL–INLAND; POH/AFM.

**Objective.** To determine that the applicant:

1. Exhibits knowledge of the elements related to water taxi and sailing procedures.
2. Positions the flight controls properly for the existing wind conditions.
3. Plans and follows the most favorable course while taxiing or sailing considering wind, water current, water conditions and maritime regulations.
4. Uses the appropriate idle, plow, or step taxi technique.
5. Uses flight controls, flaps, doors, water rudder, and power correctly so as to follow the desired course while sailing.
6. Prevents and corrects for porpoising and skipping.
7. Avoids other aircraft, vessels, and hazards.
8. Complies with seaplane base signs, signals, and clearances.

## F. TASK: BEFORE TAKEOFF CHECK (AMEL and AMES)

REFERENCES: FAA-H-8083-3; POH/AFM.

**Objective.** To determine that the applicant:

1. Exhibits knowledge of the elements related to the before takeoff check. This shall include the reasons for checking each item and how to detect malfunctions.
2. Positions the airplane properly considering other aircraft/vessel, wind and surface conditions.
3. Divides attention inside and outside the cockpit.
4. Ensures that engine temperatures and pressure are suitable for run-up and takeoff.
5. Accomplishes the before takeoff checklist and ensures the airplane is in safe operating condition.
6. Reviews takeoff performance airspeeds, takeoff distances, departures, and emergency procedures.
7. Avoids runway incursion and/or ensures no conflict with traffic prior to taxiing into takeoff position.

# III. AREA OF OPERATION: AIRPORT AND SEAPLANE BASE OPERATIONS

## A. TASK: RADIO COMMUNICATIONS AND ATC LIGHT SIGNALS (AMEL and AMES)

REFERENCES: 14 CFR part 91; AC 61-23/FAA-H-8083-25; AIM.

**Objective.** To determine that the applicant:

1. Exhibits knowledge of the elements related to radio communications and ATC light signals.
2. Selects appropriate frequencies.
3. Transmits using recommended phraseology.
4. Acknowledges radio communications and complies with instructions.

## B. TASK: TRAFFIC PATTERNS (AMEL and AMES)

REFERENCES: FAA-H-8083-3, AC 61-23/FAA-H-8083-25; AC 90-66; AIM.

**Objective.** To determine that the applicant:

1. Exhibits knowledge of the elements related to traffic patterns. This shall include procedures at airports with and without operating control towers, prevention of runway incursions, collision avoidance, wake turbulence avoidance, and wind shear.
2. Complies with proper traffic pattern procedures.
3. Maintains proper spacing from other aircraft.
4. Corrects for wind drift to maintain the proper ground track.
5. Maintains orientation with the runway/landing area in use.
6. Maintains traffic pattern altitude, ±100 feet (30 meters), and the appropriate airspeed, ±10 knots.

## C. TASK: AIRPORT/SEAPLANE BASE, RUNWAY, AND TAXIWAY SIGNS, MARKINGS, AND LIGHTING (AMEL and AMES)

REFERENCES: AC 61-23/FAA-H-8083-25; AIM.

**Objective.** To determine that the applicant:

1. Exhibits knowledge of the elements related to airport/seaplane base, runway, and taxiway operations with emphasis on runway incursion avoidance.
2. Properly identifies and interprets airport/seaplane base, runway, and taxiway signs, markings, and lighting.

# IV. AREA OF OPERATION: TAKEOFFS, LANDINGS, AND GO-AROUNDS

## A. TASK: NORMAL AND CROSSWIND TAKEOFF AND CLIMB
(AMEL and AMES)

**NOTE:** If a crosswind condition does not exist, the applicant's knowledge of crosswind elements shall be evaluated through oral testing.

REFERENCES: FAA-H-8083-3; POH/AFM.

**Objective.** To determine that the applicant:

1. Exhibits knowledge of the elements related to a normal and crosswind takeoff, climb operations, and rejected takeoff procedures.
2. Positions the flight controls for the existing wind conditions.
3. Clears the area; taxies into the takeoff position and aligns the airplane on the runway center/takeoff path.
4. Retracts the water rudders as appropriate, (AMES) advances the throttles smoothly to takeoff power.
5. Establishes and maintains the most efficient planing/lift-off attitude and corrects for porpoising and skipping (AMES).
6. Lifts off at the recommended airspeed and accelerates to $V_Y$.
7. Establishes a pitch attitude that will maintain $V_Y$ +10/-5 knots.
8. Retracts the landing gear, if appropriate, and flaps after a positive rate of climb is established.
9. Maintains takeoff power and $V_Y$ +10/-5 knots to a safe maneuvering altitude.
10. Maintains directional control and proper wind-drift correction throughout the takeoff and climb.
11. Complies with noise abatement procedures.
12. Completes the appropriate checklist.

**B. TASK: NORMAL AND CROSSWIND APPROACH AND LANDING**
(AMEL and AMES)

**NOTE:** If a crosswind condition does not exist, the applicant's knowledge of crosswind elements shall be evaluated through oral testing.

REFERENCES: FAA-H-8083-3; POH/AFM.

**Objective.** To determine that the applicant:

1. Exhibits knowledge of the elements related to a normal and crosswind approach and landing.
2. Adequately surveys the intended landing area (AMES).
3. Considers the wind conditions, landing surface, obstructions, and selects a suitable touchdown point.
4. Establishes the recommended approach and landing configuration and airspeed, and adjusts pitch attitude and power as required.
5. Maintains a stabilized approach and recommended airspeed, or in its absence, not more than 1.3 $V_{SO}$, +10/-5 knots, with wind gust factor applied.
6. Makes smooth, timely, and correct control application during the roundout and touchdown.
7. Contacts the water at the proper pitch attitude (AMES).
8. Touches down smoothly at approximate stalling speed (AMEL).
9. Touches down at or within 400 feet (120 meters) beyond a specified point, with no drift, and with the airplane's longitudinal axis aligned with and over the runway center/landing path.
10. Maintains crosswind correction and directional control throughout the approach and landing sequence.
11. Completes the appropriate checklist.

## C. TASK: SHORT-FIELD (CONFINED AREA—AMES) TAKEOFF AND MAXIMUM PERFORMANCE CLIMB (AMEL and AMES)

REFERENCES: FAA-H-8083-3; POH/AFM.

**Objective.** To determine that the applicant:

1. Exhibits knowledge of the elements related to a short-field (confined area AMES) takeoff and maximum performance climb.
2. Positions the flight controls for the existing wind conditions; sets the flaps as recommended.
3. Clears the area; taxies into takeoff position utilizing maximum available takeoff area and aligns the airplane on the runway center/take-off path.
4. Selects an appropriate take-off path for the existing conditions (AMES).
5. Applies brakes (if appropriate), while advancing the throttles smoothly to takeoff power.
6. Establishes and maintains the most efficient planing/lift-off attitude and corrects for porpoising and skipping (AMES).
7. Lifts off at the recommended airspeed, and accelerates to the recommended obstacle clearance airspeed or $V_X$.
8. Establishes a pitch attitude that will maintain the recommended obstacle clearance airspeed, or $V_X$, +10/-5 knots, until the obstacle is cleared, or until the airplane is 50 feet (20 meters) above the surface.
9. After clearing the obstacle, establishes the pitch attitude for $V_Y$ accelerates to $V_Y$, and maintains $V_Y$, +10/-5 knots, during the climb.
10. Retracts the landing gear, if appropriate, and flaps after clear of any obstacles or as recommended by manufacturer.
11. Maintains takeoff power and $V_Y$ +10/-5 knots to a safe maneuvering altitude.
12. Maintains directional control and proper wind-drift correction throughout the takeoff and climb.
13. Completes the appropriate checklist.

## D. TASK: SHORT-FIELD APPROACH (CONFINED AREA—AMES) AND LANDING (AMEL AND AMES)

REFERENCES: FAA-H-8083-3; POH/AFM.

**Objective.** To determine that the applicant:

1. Exhibits knowledge of the elements related to a short-field (confined area AMES) approach and landing.
2. Adequately surveys the intended landing area (AMES).
3. Considers the wind conditions, landing surface, obstructions, and selects the most suitable touchdown point.
4. Establishes the recommended approach and landing configuration and airspeed; adjusts pitch attitude and power as required.
5. Maintains a stabilized approach and recommended approach airspeed, or in its absence not more than 1.3 $V_{SO}$, +10/-5 knots, with wind gust factor applied.
6. Makes smooth, timely, and correct control application during the roundout and touchdown.
7. Selects the proper landing path, contacts the water at the minimum safe airspeed with the proper pitch attitude for the surface conditions (AMES).
8. Touches down smoothly at minimum control airspeed (AMEL).
9. Touches down at or within 200 feet (60 meters) beyond a specified point, with no side drift, minimum float, and with the airplane's longitudinal axis aligned with and over the runway center/landing path.
10. Maintains crosswind correction and directional control throughout the approach and landing sequence.
11. Applies brakes, (AMEL) or elevator control (AMES), as necessary, to stop in the shortest distance consistent with safety.
12. Completes the appropriate checklist.

## G. TASK: GLASSY WATER TAKEOFF AND CLIMB (AMES)

**NOTE:** If a glassy water condition does not exist, the applicant shall be evaluated by simulating the TASK.

REFERENCES: FAA-H-8083-3; POH/AFM.

**Objective.** To determine that the applicant:

1. Exhibits knowledge of the elements related to glassy water takeoff and climb.
2. Positions the flight controls and flaps for the existing conditions.
3. Clears the area; selects an appropriate takeoff path considering surface hazards and/or vessels and surface conditions.
4. Retracts the water rudders as appropriate; advances the throttle smoothly to takeoff power.
5. Establishes and maintains an appropriate planing attitude, directional control, and corrects for porpoising, skipping, and increases in water drag.
6. Utilizes appropriate techniques to lift seaplane from the water considering surface conditions.
7. Establishes proper attitude/airspeed, and accelerates to $V_Y$, +10/-5 knots during the climb.
8. Retracts the landing gear, if appropriate, and flaps after a positive rate of climb is established.
9. Maintains takeoff power and $V_Y$ +10/-5 knots to a safe maneuvering altitude.
10. Maintains directional control and proper wind-drift correction throughout takeoff and climb.
11. Completes the appropriate checklist.

## H. TASK: GLASSY WATER APPROACH AND LANDING (AMES)

**NOTE:** If a glassy water condition does not exist, the applicant shall be evaluated by simulating the TASK.

REFERENCES: FAA-H-8083-3; POH/AFM.

**Objective.** To determine that the applicant:

1. Exhibits knowledge of the elements related to glassy water approach and landing.
2. Adequately surveys the intended landing area.
3. Considers the wind conditions, water depth, hazards, surrounding terrain, and other watercraft.
4. Selects the most suitable approach path and touchdown area.
5. Establishes the recommended approach and landing configuration and airspeed, and adjusts pitch attitude and power as required.
6. Maintains a stabilized approach and the recommended approach airspeed, +10/-5 knots and maintains a touchdown pitch attitude and descent rate from the last altitude reference until touchdown.
7. Makes smooth, timely, and correct power and control adjustments to maintain proper pitch attitude and rate of descent to touchdown.
8. Contacts the water in the proper pitch attitude, and slows to idle taxi speed.
9. Maintains crosswind correction and directional control throughout the approach and landing sequence.
10. Completes the appropriate checklist.

## I. TASK: ROUGH WATER TAKEOFF AND CLIMB (AMES)

**NOTE:** If a rough water condition does not exist, the applicant shall be evaluated by simulating the TASK.

REFERENCES: FAA-H-8083-3; POH/AFM.

**Objective.** To determine that the applicant:

1. Exhibits knowledge of the elements related to rough water takeoff and climb.
2. Positions the flight controls and flaps for the existing conditions.
3. Clears the area; selects an appropriate takeoff path considering wind, swells, surface hazards, and/or vessels.
4. Retracts the water rudders as appropriate; advances the throttle smoothly to takeoff power.
5. Establishes and maintains an appropriate planing attitude, directional control, and corrects for porpoising, skipping, or excessive bouncing.
6. Lifts off at minimum airspeed and accelerates to $V_Y$, +10/-5 knots before leaving ground effect.
7. Retracts the landing gear, if appropriate, and flaps after a positive rate of climb is established.
8. Maintains takeoff power and $V_Y$ +10/-5 knots to a safe maneuvering altitude.
9. Maintains directional control and proper wind-drift correction throughout takeoff and climb.
10. Completes the appropriate checklist.

## J. TASK: ROUGH WATER APPROACH AND LANDING (AMES)

**NOTE:** If a rough water condition does not exist, the applicant shall be evaluated by simulating the TASK.

REFERENCES: FAA-H-8083-3; POH/AFM.

**Objective.** To determine that the applicant:

1. Exhibits knowledge of the elements related to rough water approach and landing.
2. Adequately surveys the intended landing area.
3. Considers the wind conditions, water, depth, hazards, surrounding terrain, and other watercraft.
4. Selects the most suitable approach path, and touchdown area.
5. Establishes the recommended approach and landing configuration and airspeed, and adjusts pitch attitude and power as required.
6. Maintains a stabilized approach and the recommended approach airspeed, or in its absence not more than 1.3 $V_{SO}$ +10/-5 knots with wind gust factor applied.
7. Makes smooth, timely, and correct power and control application during the roundout and touch down.
8. Contacts the water in the proper pitch attitude, and at the proper airspeed, considering the type of rough water.
9. Maintains crosswind correction and directional control throughout the approach and landing sequence.
10. Completes the appropriate checklist.

## K. TASK: GO-AROUND/REJECTED LANDING (AMEL and AMES)

REFERENCES: FAA-H-8083-3; POH/AFM.

**Objective.** To determine that the applicant:

1. Exhibits knowledge of the elements related to a go-around/rejected landing.
2. Makes a timely decision to discontinue the approach to landing.
3. Applies takeoff power immediately and transitions to climb pitch attitude for $V_Y$ and maintains $V_Y$ +10/-5 knots.
4. Retracts the flaps, as appropriate.
5. Retracts the landing gear, if appropriate, after a positive rate of climb is established.
6. Maneuvers to the side of the runway/landing area to clear and avoid conflicting traffic.
7. Maintains takeoff power and $V_Y$ +10/-5 knots to a safe maneuvering altitude.
8. Maintains directional control and proper wind-drift correction throughout the climb.
9. Completes the appropriate checklist.

# V. AREA OF OPERATION: PERFORMANCE MANEUVER

**TASK: STEEP TURNS** (AMEL and AMES)

REFERENCES: FAA-H-8083-3; POH/AFM.

**Objective.** To determine that the applicant:

1. Exhibits knowledge of the elements related to steep turns.
2. Establishes the manufacturer's recommended airspeed or if one is not stated, a safe airspeed not to exceed $V_A$.
3. Rolls into a coordinated 360° turn; maintains a 45° bank.
4. Performs the task in the opposite direction, as specified by the examiner.
5. Divides attention between airplane control and orientation.
6. Maintains the entry altitude, ±100 feet (30 meters), airspeed, ±10 knots, bank, ±5°; and rolls out on the entry heading, ±10°.

## VI. AREA OF OPERATION: GROUND REFERENCE MANEUVERS

**NOTE:** The examiner shall select at least one TASK.

### A. TASK: RECTANGULAR COURSE (AMEL and AMES)

REFERENCE: FAA-H-8083-3.

**Objective.** To determine that the applicant:

1. Exhibits knowledge of the elements related to a rectangular course.
2. Selects a suitable reference area.
3. Plans the maneuver so as to enter a left or right pattern, 600 to 1,000 feet AGL (180 to 300 meters) at an appropriate distance from the selected reference area, 45° to the downwind leg.
4. Applies adequate wind-drift correction during straight-and-turning flight to maintain a constant ground track around the rectangular reference area.
5. Divides attention between airplane control and the ground track while maintaining coordinated flight.
6. Maintains altitude, ±100 feet (30 meters); maintains airspeed, ±10 knots.

### B. TASK: S-TURNS (AMEL and AMES)

REFERENCE: FAA-H-8083-3.

**Objective.** To determine that the applicant:

1. Exhibits knowledge of the elements related to S-turns.
2. Selects a suitable ground reference line.
3. Plans the maneuver so as to enter at 600 to 1,000 feet (180 to 300 meters) AGL, perpendicular to the selected reference line.
4. Applies adequate wind-drift correction to track a constant radius turn on each side of the selected reference line.
5. Reverses the direction of turn directly over the selected reference line.
6. Divides attention between airplane control and the ground track while maintaining coordinated flight.
7. Maintains altitude, ±100 feet (30 meters); maintains airspeed, ±10 knots.

**C. TASK: TURNS AROUND A POINT** (AMEL and AMES)

REFERENCE: FAA-H-8083-3.

**Objective.** To determine that the applicant:

1. Exhibits knowledge of the elements related to turns around a point.
2. Selects a suitable ground reference point.
3. Plans the maneuver so as to enter left or right at 600 to 1,000 feet (180 to 300 meters) AGL, at an appropriate distance from the reference point.
4. Applies adequate wind-drift correction to track a constant radius turn around the selected reference point.
5. Divides attention between airplane control and the ground track while maintaining coordinated flight.
6. Maintains altitude, ±100 feet (30 meters); maintains airspeed, ±10 knots.

# VII. AREA OF OPERATION: NAVIGATION

## A. TASK: PILOTAGE AND DEAD RECKONING (AMEL and AMES)

REFERENCE: AC 61-23/FAA-H-8083-25.

**Objective.** To determine that the applicant:

1. Exhibits knowledge of the elements related to pilotage and dead reckoning.
2. Follows the preplanned course by reference to landmarks.
3. Identifies landmarks by relating surface features to chart symbols.
4. Navigates by means of precomputed headings, groundspeeds, and elapsed time.
5. Corrects for and records the differences between preflight groundspeed, and heading calculations and those determined en route.
6. Verifies the airplane's position within three (3) nautical miles of the flight-planned route.
7. Arrives at the en route checkpoints within five (5) minutes of the initial or revised ETA and provides a destination estimate.
8. Maintains the appropriate altitude, ±200 feet (60 meters) and heading, ±15°.

## B. TASK: NAVIGATION SYSTEMS AND RADAR SERVICES
(AMEL and AMES)

REFERENCES: FAA-H-8083-3, AC 61-23/FAA-H-8083-25; Navigation Equipment Operation Manuals, AIM.

**Objective.** To determine that the applicant:

1. Exhibits knowledge of the elements related to navigation systems and radar services.
2. Demonstrates the ability to use an airborne electronic navigation system.
3. Locates the airplane's position using the navigation system.
4. Intercepts and tracks a given course, radial or bearing, as appropriate.
5. Recognizes and describes the indication of station passage, if appropriate.
6. Recognizes signal loss and takes appropriate action.
7. Uses proper communication procedures when utilizing radar services.
8. Maintains the appropriate altitude, ±200 feet (60 meters) and heading ±15°.

## C. TASK: DIVERSION (AMEL and AMES)

REFERENCES: FAA-H-8083-25; AIM.

**Objective.** To determine that the applicant:

1. Exhibits knowledge of the elements related to diversion.
2. Selects an appropriate alternate airport and route.
3. Makes an accurate estimate of heading, groundspeed, arrival time, and fuel consumption to the alternate airport.
4. Maintains the appropriate altitude, ±200 feet (60 meters) and headings, ±15°.

## D. TASK: LOST PROCEDURES (AMEL and AMES)

REFERENCES: FAA-H-8083-25; AIM.

**Objective.** To determine that the applicant:

1. Exhibits knowledge of the elements related to lost procedures.
2. Selects an appropriate course of action.
3. Maintains an appropriate heading and climbs, if necessary.
4. Identifies prominent landmarks.
5. Uses navigation systems/facilities and/or contacts an ATC facility for assistance, as appropriate.

# VIII. AREA OF OPERATION: SLOW FLIGHT AND STALLS

## A. TASK: MANEUVERING DURING SLOW FLIGHT (AMEL and AMES)

REFERENCES: FAA-H-8083-3; POH/AFM.

**Objective.** To determine that the applicant:

1. Exhibits knowledge of the elements related to maneuvering during slow flight.
2. Selects an entry altitude that will allow the task to be completed no lower than 3,000 feet (920 meters) AGL.
3. Establishes and maintains an airspeed at which any further increase in angle of attack, increase in load factor, or reduction in power, would result in an immediate stall.
4. Accomplishes coordinated straight-and-level flight, turns, climbs, and descents with landing gear and flap configurations specified by the examiner.
5. Divides attention between airplane control and orientation.
6. Maintains the specified altitude, ±100 feet (30 meters); specified heading, ±10°; airspeed, +10/–0 knots and specified angle of bank, ±10°.

## B. TASK: POWER-OFF STALLS (AMEL and AMES)

REFERENCES: FAA-H-8083-3, AC 61-67; POH/AFM

**Objective.** To determine that the applicant:

1. Exhibits knowledge of the elements related to power-off stalls.
2. Selects an entry altitude that allows the task to be completed no lower than 3,000 feet (460 meters) AGL.
3. Establishes a stabilized descent in the approach or landing configuration, as specified by the examiner.
4. Transitions smoothly from the approach or landing attitude to a pitch attitude that will induce a stall.
5. Maintains a specified heading, ±10°, in straight flight; maintains a specified angle of bank not to exceed 20°, ±10°; in turning flight, while inducing the stall.
6. Recognizes and recovers promptly after a stall occurs by simultaneously reducing the angle of attack, increasing power to maximum allowable, and leveling the wings to return to a straight-and-level flight attitude with a minimum loss of altitude appropriate for the airplane.
7. Retracts the flaps to the recommended setting; retracts the landing gear, if retractable, after a positive rate of climb is established.
8. Accelerates to $V_X$ or $V_Y$ speed before the final flap retraction; returns to the altitude, heading, and airspeed specified by the examiner.

## C. TASK: POWER-ON STALLS (AMEL and AMES)

**NOTE:** In some high performance airplanes the power setting may have to be reduced below the practical test standards guideline power setting to prevent excessively high pitch attitudes (greater than 30° nose up).

REFERENCES: FAA-H-8083-3, AC 61-67; POH/AFM.

**Objective.** To determine that the applicant:

1. Exhibits knowledge of the elements related to power-on stalls.
2. Selects an entry altitude that allows the task to be completed no lower than 3,000 feet (460 meters) AGL.
3. Establishes the takeoff or departure configuration. Sets power to no less than 65 percent available power.
4. Transitions smoothly from the takeoff or departure attitude to the pitch attitude that will induce a stall.
5. Maintains a specified heading, ±10°, in straight flight; maintains a specified angle of bank not to exceed 20°, ±10°, in turning flight, while inducing the stall.
6. Recognizes and recovers promptly after the stall occurs by simultaneously reducing the angle of attack, increasing power to maximum allowable, and leveling the wings to return to a straight-and-level flight attitude with a minimum loss of altitude appropriate for the airplane.
7. Retracts the flaps to the recommended setting; retracts the landing gear if retractable, after a positive rate of climb is established.
8. Accelerates to $V_X$ or $V_Y$ speed before the final flap retraction; returns to the altitude, heading, and airspeed specified by the examiner.

## D. TASK: SPIN AWARENESS (AMEL and AMES)

REFERENCES: FAA-H-8083-3, AC 61-67; POH/AFM.

**Objective.** To determine that the applicant exhibits knowledge of the elements related to spin awareness by explaining:

1. Aerodynamic factors related to spins.
2. Flight situations where unintentional spins may occur.
3. Procedures for recovery from unintentional spins.

# IX. AREA OF OPERATION: BASIC INSTRUMENT MANEUVERS

**NOTE:** The examiner shall select TASK E and at least two other TASKs. If the applicant holds an instrument rating airplane he or she only needs to demonstrate TASK E.

## A. TASK: STRAIGHT-AND-LEVEL FLIGHT (AMEL and AMES)

REFERENCES: FAA-H-8083-3, FAA-H-8083-15.

**Objective.** To determine that the applicant:

1. Exhibits knowledge of the elements related to attitude instrument flying during straight-and-level flight.
2. Maintains straight-and-level flight solely by reference to instruments using proper instrument cross-check and interpretation, and coordinated control application.
3. Maintains altitude, ±200 feet (60 meters); heading, ±20°; and airspeed, ±10 knots.

## B. TASK: CONSTANT AIRSPEED CLIMBS (AMEL and AMES)

REFERENCES: FAA-H-8083-3, FAA-H-8083-15.

**Objective.** To determine that the applicant:

1. Exhibits knowledge of the elements related to attitude instrument flying during constant airspeed climbs.
2. Establishes the climb configuration specified by the examiner.
3. Transitions to the climb pitch attitude and power setting on an assigned heading using proper instrument cross-check and interpretation, and coordinated control application.
4. Demonstrates climbs solely by reference to instruments at a constant airspeed to specific altitudes in straight flight and turns.
5. Levels off at the assigned altitude and maintains that altitude, ±200 feet (60 meters); maintains heading, ±20°; maintains airspeed, ±10 knots.

## C. TASK: CONSTANT AIRSPEED DESCENTS (AMEL and AMES)

REFERENCES: FAA-H-8083-3, FAA-H-8083-15.

**Objective.** To determine that the applicant:

1. Exhibits knowledge of the elements related to attitude instrument flying during constant airspeed descents.
2. Establishes the descent configuration specified by the examiner.
3. Transitions to the descent pitch attitude and power setting on an assigned heading using proper instrument cross-check and interpretation, and coordinated control application.
4. Demonstrates descents solely by reference to instruments at a constant airspeed to specific altitudes in straight flight and turns.
5. Levels off at the assigned altitude and maintains that altitude, ±200 feet (60 meters); maintains heading, ±20°; maintains airspeed, ±10 knots.

## D. TASK: TURNS TO HEADINGS (AMEL and AMES)

REFERENCES: FAA-H-8083-3, FAA-H-8083-15.

**Objective.** To determine that the applicant:

1. Exhibits knowledge of the elements related to attitude instrument flying during turns to headings.
2. Transitions to the level-turn attitude using proper instrument cross-check and interpretation, and coordinated control application.
3. Demonstrates turns to headings solely by reference to instruments; maintains altitude, ±200 feet (60 meters); maintains a standard rate turn and rolls out on the assigned heading, ±10°; maintains airspeed, ±10 knots.

## E. TASK: RECOVERY FROM UNUSUAL FLIGHT ATTITUDES
(AMEL and AMES)

REFERENCES: FAA-H-8083-3, FAA-H-8083-15.

**Objective.** To determine that the applicant:

1. Exhibits knowledge of the elements related to attitude instrument flying during unusual attitudes.
2. Recognizes unusual flight attitudes solely by reference to instruments; recovers promptly to a stabilized level flight attitude using proper instrument cross-check and interpretation and smooth, coordinated control application in the correct sequence.

**F. TASK: RADIO COMMUNICATIONS, NAVIGATION SYSTEMS/FACILITIES, AND RADAR SERVICES** (AMEL and AMES)

REFERENCES: AC 61-23/FAA-H-8083-25, FAA-H-8083-3, FAA-H-8083-15.

**Objective.** To determine that the applicant:

1. Exhibits knowledge of the elements related to radio communications, navigation systems/facilities, and radar services available for use during flight solely by reference to instruments.
2. Selects the proper frequency and identifies the appropriate facility.
3. Follows verbal instructions and/or navigation systems/facilities for guidance.
4. Determines the minimum safe altitude.
5. Maintains altitude, ±200 feet (60 meters); maintains heading, ±20°; maintains airspeed, ±10 knots.

# X. AREA OF OPERATION: EMERGENCY OPERATIONS

**NOTE:** Examiners shall select an entry altitude that will allow the single engine demonstrations task to be completed no lower than 3,000 feet (920 meters) AGL or the manufacturer's recommended altitude, whichever is higher. At altitudes lower than 3,000 feet (920 meters) AGL, engine failure shall be simulated by reducing throttle to idle and then establishing zero thrust.

## A. TASK: EMERGENCY DESCENT (AMEL and AMES)

REFERENCES: FAA-H-8083-3; POH/AFM.

**Objective.** To determine that the applicant:

1. Exhibits knowledge of the elements related to an emergency descent.
2. Recognizes situations, such as depressurization, cockpit smoke and/or fire that require an emergency descent.
3. Establishes the appropriate airspeed and configuration for the emergency descent.
4. Exhibits orientation, division of attention, and proper planning.
5. Maintains positive load factors during the descent.
6. Completes appropriate checklists.

## B. TASK: ENGINE FAILURE DURING TAKEOFF BEFORE $V_{MC}$ (SIMULATED—AMEL and AMES)

REFERENCES: FAA-H-8083-3; POH/AFM.

**NOTE:** Engine failure (simulated) shall be accomplished before reaching 50 percent of the calculated $V_{MC}$.

**Objective.** To determine that the applicant:

1. Exhibits knowledge of the elements related to the procedure used for engine failure during takeoff prior to reaching $V_{MC}$.
2. Closes the throttles smoothly and promptly when simulated engine failure occurs.
3. Maintains directional control and applies brakes (AMEL) or flight controls (AMES), as necessary.

## C. TASK: ENGINE FAILURE AFTER LIFT-OFF (SIMULATED—AMEL and AMES)

REFERENCES: FAA-H-8083-3; POH/AFM.

**Objective.** To determine that the applicant:

1. Exhibits knowledge of the elements related to the procedure used for engine failure after lift-off.
2. Recognizes a simulated engine failure promptly, maintains control, and utilizes appropriate emergency procedures.
3. Reduces drag, identifies and verifies the inoperative engine after simulated engine failure.
4. Simulates feathering the propeller on the inoperative engine. Examiner shall then establish zero-thrust on the inoperative engine.
5. Establishes $V_{YSE}$; if obstructions are present, establishes $V_{XSE}$ or $V_{MC}$ +5 knots, whichever is greater, until obstructions are cleared. Then. transitions to $V_{YSE}$.
6. Banks toward the operating engine as required for best performance.
7. Monitors operating engine and makes adjustments as necessary.
8. Recognizes the airplane's performance capabilities. If a climb is not possible at $V_{YSE}$, maintain $V_{YSE}$ and return to the departure airport for landing, or initiates an approach to the most suitable landing area available.
9. Secures the (simulated) inoperative engine.
10. Maintains heading, ±10°, and airspeed, ±5 knots.
11. Completes appropriate emergency checklist.

## D. TASK: APPROACH AND LANDING WITH AN INOPERATIVE ENGINE (SIMULATED—AMEL and AMES)

REFERENCES: FAA-H-8083-3; POH/AFM.

**Objective.** To determine that the applicant:

1. Exhibits knowledge of the elements related to an approach and landing with an engine inoperative to include engine failure on final approach.
2. Recognizes engine failure and takes appropriate action, maintains control, and utilizes recommended emergency procedures.
3. Banks toward the operating engine, as required, for best performance.
4. Monitors the operating engine and makes adjustments as necessary.
5. Maintains the recommended approach airspeed +10/–5, and landing configuration with a stabilized approach, until landing is assured.
6. Makes smooth, timely and correct control applications during roundout and touchdown.
7. Touches down on the first one-third of available runway, with no drift and the airplane's longitudinal axis aligned with and over the runway center/landing path.
8. Maintains crosswind correction and directional control throughout the approach and landing sequence.
9. Completes appropriate checklists.

## E. TASK: SYSTEMS AND EQUIPMENT MALFUNCTIONS
(AMEL and AMES)

REFERENCES: FAA-H-8083-3; POH/AFM.

**Objective.** To determine that the applicant:

1. Exhibits knowledge of the elements related to system and equipment malfunctions appropriate to the airplane provided for the practical test.
2. Analyzes the situation and takes the appropriate action for simulated emergencies appropriate to the airplane provided for the practical test for at least three (3) of the following:

   a. partial or complete power loss.
   b. engine roughness or overheat.
   c. carburetor or induction icing.
   d. loss of oil pressure.
   e. fuel starvation.
   f. electrical malfunction.
   g. vacuum/pressure, and associated flight instruments malfunction.
   h. pitot/static.
   i. landing gear or flap malfunction.
   j. inoperative trim.
   k. inadvertent door or window opening.
   l. structural icing.
   m. smoke/fire/engine compartment fire.
   n. any other emergency appropriate to the airplane.

3. Follows the appropriate checklist or procedure.

## F. TASK: EMERGENCY EQUIPMENT AND SURVIVAL GEAR
(AMEL and AMES)

REFERENCES: FAA-H-8083-3; POH/AFM.

**Objective.** To determine that the applicant:

Exhibits knowledge of the elements related to emergency equipment and survival gear appropriate to the airplane and environment encountered during flight. Identifies appropriate equipment that should be aboard the airplane.

# XI. AREA OF OPERATION:  MULTIENGINE OPERATIONS

**NOTE:** If the applicant is instrument rated, and has previously demonstrated instrument proficiency in a multiengine airplane or does not hold an instrument rating airplane, TASKS D and C need not be accomplished

## A.  TASK:  MANEUVERING WITH ONE ENGINE INOPERATIVE
(AMEL and AMES)

REFERENCES:  FAA-H-8083-3; POH/AFM.

**NOTE:** The feathering of one propeller shall be demonstrated in flight, in a multiengine airplane equipped with propellers which can be safely feathered and unfeathered. The maneuver shall be performed at altitudes and positions where safe landings on established airports can be readily accomplished. In the event a propeller cannot be unfeathered during the practical test, it shall be treated as an emergency.

**Objective.** To determine that the applicant:

1.  Exhibits knowledge of the elements related to maneuvering with one engine inoperative.
2.  Recognizes engine failure and maintains control.
3.  Sets the engine controls, reduces drag, identifies and verifies the inoperative engine, and feathers appropriate propeller.
4.  Establishes and maintains a bank toward the operating engine as required for best performance in straight and level flight.
5.  Follows the prescribed checklists to verify procedures for securing the inoperative engine.
6.  Monitors the operating engine and makes necessary adjustments.
7.  Demonstrates coordinated flight with one engine inoperative (propeller feathered).
8.  Restarts the inoperative engine using appropriate restart procedures.
9.  Maintains altitude ±100 feet (30 meters) or minimum sink as appropriate and heading ±10°.
10.  Completes the appropriate checklists.

## B. TASK: $V_{MC}$ DEMONSTRATION (AMEL and AMES)

REFERENCES: FAA-H-8083-3; POH/AFM.

**NOTE 1**: An applicant seeking a airplane—multiengine land (AMEL) rating, "Limited to Center Thrust," is not required to be evaluated on this TASK.

**NOTE 2**: Airplanes with normally aspirated engines will lose power as altitude increases because of the reduced density of the air entering the induction system of the engine. This loss of power will result in a $V_{MC}$ lower than the stall speed at higher altitudes. Therefore, recovery should be made at the first indication of loss of directional control, stall warning, or buffet.

Do not perform this maneuver by increasing the pitch attitude to a high angle with both engines operating and then reducing power on the critical engine. This technique is hazardous and may result in loss of airplane control.

**Objective.** To determine that the applicant:

1. Exhibits knowledge of the elements related to $V_{MC}$ by explaining the causes of loss of directional controls at airspeeds less than $V_{MC}$, the factors affecting $V_{MC}$ and the safe recovery procedures.
2. Configures the airplane at $V_{SSE}/V_{YSE}$, as appropriate—

   a. Landing gear retracted.
   b. Flaps set for takeoff.
   c. Cowl flaps set for takeoff.
   d. Trim set for takeoff.
   e. Propellers set for high RPM.
   f. Power on critical engine reduced to idle.
   g. Power on operating engine set to takeoff or maximum available power.

3. Establishes a single-engine climb attitude with the airspeed at approximately 10 knots above $V_{SSE}$.
4. Establishes a bank toward the operating engine, as required for best performance and controllability.
5. Increases the pitch attitude slowly to reduce the airspeed at approximately 1 knot per second while applying rudder pressure to maintain directional control until full rudder is applied.
6. Recognizes indications of loss of directional control, stall warning or buffet.

7. Recovers promptly by simultaneously reducing power sufficiently on the operating engine while decreasing the angle of attack as necessary to regain airspeed and directional control. Recovery SHOULD NOT be attempted by increasing the power on the simulated failed engine.

8. Recovers within 20° of the entry heading.

9. Advances power smoothly on operating engine and accelerates to $V_{XSE}/V_{YSE}$, as appropriate, +10/−5 knots, during the recovery.

## C. TASK: ENGINE FAILURE DURING FLIGHT (By Reference to Instruments) (AMEL and AMES)

REFERENCES: 14 CFR part 61; FAA-H-8083-3, FAA-H-8083-15.

**Objective.** To determine that the applicant:

1. Exhibits knowledge of the elements by explaining the procedures used during instrument flight with one engine inoperative.

2. Recognizes engine failure, sets the engine controls, reduces drag, identifies, and verifies the inoperative engine and feathers appropriate engine propeller.

3. Establishes and maintains a bank toward the operating engine as required for best performance in straight and level.

4. Follows the prescribed checklists to verify procedures for securing the inoperative engine.

5. Monitors the operating engine and makes necessary adjustments.

6. Demonstrates coordinated flight with one engine inoperative.

7. Maintains altitude ±100 feet (30 meters), or minimum sink as appropriate and heading ±10°, bank ±5°, and levels off from climbs and descents within ± 100 feet (30 meters).

## D. TASK: INSTRUMENT APPROACH—ONE ENGINE INOPERATIVE (By Reference to Instruments) (AMEL and AMES)

REFERENCES: 14 CFR part 61; FAA-H-8083-3, AC 61-27; FAA-S-8081-4.

**Objective.** To determine that the applicant:

1. Exhibits knowledge of the elements by explaining the procedures used during a published instrument approach with one engine inoperative.
2. Recognizes engine failure, sets the engine controls, reduces drag, identifies and verifies the inoperative engine, and feathers appropriate engine propeller.
3. Establishes and maintains a bank toward the operating engine, as required, for best performance in straight and level flight.
4. Follows the prescribed checklists to verify procedures for securing the inoperative engine.
5. Monitors the operating engine and makes necessary adjustments.
6. Requests and receives an actual or a simulated ATC clearance for an instrument approach.
7. Follows the actual or a simulated ATC clearance for an instrument approach.
8. Maintains altitude within 100 feet (30 meters), the airspeed within ±10 knots if within the aircraft's capability, and heading ±10.
9. Establishes a rate of descent that will ensure arrival at the MDA or DH/DA, with the airplane in a position from which a descent to a landing, on the intended runway can be made, either straight in or circling as appropriate.
10. On final approach segment, no more than three-quarter-scale deflection of the CDI/glide slope indicator. For RMI or ADF indicators, within 10° of the course.
11. Avoids loss of aircraft control, or attempted flight contrary to the engine-inoperative operating limitations of the aircraft.
12. Complies with the published criteria for the aircraft approach category when circling.
13. Completes landing and appropriate checklists.

# XII. AREA OF OPERATION: NIGHT OPERATION

TASK: **NIGHT PREPARATION** (AMEL and AMES)

REFERENCES: FAA-H-8083-3, AC 61-23/FAA-H-8083-25, AC 67-2; AIM, POH/AFM.

**Objective.** To determine that the applicant exhibits knowledge of the elements related to night operations by explaining:

1. Physiological aspects of night flying as it relates to vision.
2. Lighting systems identifying airports, runways, taxiways and obstructions, and pilot controlled lighting.
3. Airplane lighting systems.
4. Personal equipment essential for night flight.
5. Night orientation, navigation, and chart reading techniques.
6. Safety precautions and emergencies unique to night flying.

    FAA-S-8081-14A

# XIII. AREA OF OPERATION:  POSTFLIGHT PROCEDURES

**NOTE:**  The examiner shall select TASK A and for AMES applicants at least one other TASK.

## A. TASK:  AFTER LANDING, PARKING, AND SECURING (AMEL and AMES)

REFERENCES:  FAA-H-8083-3; POH/AFM.

**Objective.**  To determine that the applicant:

1. Exhibits knowledge of the elements related to after landing, parking and securing procedures.
2. Maintains directional control after touchdown while decelerating to an appropriate speed.
3. Observes runway hold lines and other surface control markings and lighting.
4. Parks in an appropriate area, considering the safety of nearby persons and property.
5. Follows the appropriate procedure for engine shutdown.
6. Completes the appropriate checklist.
7. Conducts an appropriate postflight inspection and secures the aircraft.

## B. TASK:  ANCHORING (AMES)

REFERENCES:  FAA-H-8083-3; POH/AFM.

**Objective.**  To determine that the applicant:

1. Exhibits knowledge of the elements related to anchoring.
2. Selects a suitable area for anchoring, considering seaplane movement, water depth, tide, wind, and weather changes.
3. Uses an adequate number of anchors and lines of sufficient strength and length to ensure the seaplane's security.

## C. TASK:  DOCKING AND MOORING (AMES)

REFERENCES:  FAA-H-8083-3; POH/AFM.

**Objective.**  To determine that the applicant:

1. Exhibits knowledge of the elements related to docking and mooring.
2. Approaches the dock or mooring buoy in the proper direction considering speed, hazards, wind, and water current.
3. Ensures seaplane security.

## D. TASK: RAMPING/BEACHING (AMES)

REFERENCES: FAA-H-8083-3; POH/AFM.

**Objective.** To determine that the applicant:

1. Exhibits knowledge of the elements related to ramping/beaching.
2. Approaches the ramp/beach considering persons and property, in the proper attitude and direction, at a safe speed, considering water depth, tide, current, and wind.
3. Ramps/beaches and secures the seaplane in a manner that will protect it from the harmful effect of wind, waves, and changes in water level.